AF504394

BY
PATRICIA EMRIE HILTON

ILLUSTRATIONS BY
gail emrie

For my children, Holly, Nikki, Ryan, DJ and Barron.
My grandchildren, Henry, Brodie, Lexi, Alex,
Jacob, Noah, Emrie, Ellie Jane and my
great grandson, Sawyer.

A big thank you hug to my husband, Denny Hilton,
my brother, Danny Emrie and my cousin, Gail Emrie.
This book would not have
been possible without their help.

Introduction

Poor Pitiful Pearl was a doll made in the 1950's by the toy company Brookglad in Brooklyn, New York.

My dear Momma and Daddy bought her for me, which I still have to this day. I drug her everywhere I went. We went to soda fountains downtown, movies, swimming pools, parks and shopping. She rode in a little basket on my bike. The most important place she went with me was my imagination. I had two brothers who referred to me as their "Kid Sister", instead of Patricia Mae, my given name at birth. They never played with me and were quick to point out they never would.

Patty Mae & Pearl

Despite that, Pearl and I had a wonderful childhood. Poor Pitiful Pearl became the sister I never had. These are our stories of the summer of 1958, Springfield, Mo.

3

Preface

During the mid 1950's I was a small little girl with big ideas. On most days I would go downtown on my bicycle. My pup, Lazy, was behind me willing, to go wherever, whenever I wanted. We went to see my momma and daddy who worked downtown. We watched the people there live their lives. We went to movies, parks, shops, cafes and soda fountains. The pup, Lazy, always waited patiently, never moving far from my bicycle.

For my birthday I adopted Pearl, a birthday gift. Then the three of us went everywhere together. The places in this book are real. The characters are my family.

This book was written to honor my parents Harlo and LaVera Audrey, Steve and Dan Emrie. No little girl could have had a happier childhood and family. Only Danny the tortoise and I survive and of course Pearl.

I wrote this book for my children Holly, Nikki, Ryan, DJ and Barron. My grandchildren Henry, Brodie, Lexi, Alex, Jacob, Noah, Emrie, Ellie Jane and my great grandson Sawyer.

While I mentioned in the book my brother Dan wouldn't play with me as a child, he has been a loving, giving big brother who I absolutely adore. As a life-long professional photographer his expert technical skills were severely abused in getting this book finished. Unfortunately, Steve (the bear) resides in heaven. This book couldn't have been written without the encouragement and loving words from my husband Denny. He is my world!

My cousin, Gail Emrie, brought the characters in this book to life through her amazing art work and wonderful sketches. She loved the project from the beginning and I will forever be indebted to her. Thank you, Gail!

For everyone who played a part in this little book, thank you from the bottom of my heart. I love you all!

Life Lessons of an 8 Year Old

I was as close to Pearl as any sister could ever be. She had reddish blonde straight hair, long legs for her size and a fair complexion.

I had dark short, curly hair an olive complexion and freckles. Pearl made our relationship easy and complicated, still we were very connected to one another.

We lived on a street named Normal, which wasn't normal at all!

It was at this time in our lives, 1958, that we met Stevie. I was 8 years old; Pearl was 4. We don't know how old Stevie was, all we knew was Stevie was a really, really big bear.

I remember the date because our parents had a concrete patio poured off the laundry room. Pearl and I put the date with our handprints in the wet cement.

Pearl said we would live forever, as long as our handprints stayed there. But she said if a hurricane took the concrete up she wasn't sure how long we would live. Her thinking was if a hurricane came down our street that we were doomed! Everything would be washed away, and that is Pearl, always thinking up stupid stuff. We live in the middle of the United States....a hurricane? Really?

Daddy bought Pearl a new flashlight. She was so excited, waving it around like she was on a runway at an airport bringing in planes. More than once, she hit me in the head with the darn thing! I wish Daddy had never given it to her.

She keeps it in a holster on her hip like Jesse James ready for a shoot out, so it is always available and when she gets excited, out it comes, waving it and jabbering in what seems a foreign language all at the same time.

She looks crazy, and I am embarrassed! Isn't that what little sisters do? They make your face turn red, your heart beat out of your chest and if you could just hide somewhere so that people didn't know she was your little sister!

Pearl would also lie when the truth fit better. She told BIG stories all the time. Momma & Daddy did not believe her, and when she would not admit it was one of her big stories, she would be put in "time out". No matter how I tried to calm her down she would cry, wave that darn flashlight and fall to the floor. The reason for telling you about Pearl is because when she does all this stupid, silly stuff, it makes it easier for me to hide the truth by calling her "a liar".

"I want bacon," said Pearl, "I'm hungry."

"Pearl, Momma doesn't have time to make bacon this morning. She will be late for work, and Daddy's already gone with an appointment to sell insurance. We're gonna have Frosted

Flakes. It's easy, and we can clean up our dishes faster than making bacon."

Pearl stomped her foot and kicked the air. "I could just kick you," she said. Oh boy! The drama queen has already gotten in her mood early this morning.

After our breakfast, which Pearl called awful, we started our adventure to the creek. It was named Fassnight Creek...but we don't know how it got that name, and Pearl thought it was a stupid name for a creek.

Stevie and the Creek

The creek was within walking distance of our house. Pearl and I would walk to the creek a lot during the hot midwestern summers. Even the fireflies would seem to hang in the air. The humidity was so thick you could cut it with a knife.

The creek had a small island in it with a tall weeping willow tree right smack in the middle. Its branches touched the creek. A beautiful green moss covered most of the island and the rocks surrounding it. The smell of the fresh mint that grew on that little island was strong and wonderful. It would be baked into our mud pies that dried in the sun.

Pearl would sit at the creeks edge and yell "Crawdad" at me as I waded out among the rocks. We would put them in a tin can from home. They would be tasty with our pies.

During heavy rains, the creek filled quickly and would carry Pearl and me off if it were not for the sure-footed steps we carefully took.

The creek ran through our little town, but further down the creek, it emptied into the storm drains. You didn't want to end up underwater and under Springfield. We would be M.I.A. (missing in action). Pearl said even her flashlight could not save us. She was right.

Most days in the summer, the creek had just a small little current, just enough to keep the water moving.

It was on one of these daily journey's that we came upon Stevie. He had come out of the wooded area at the edge of the creek. He was drinking from the creek and crying big bear tears. Pearl and I would have been scared, but he was so sad.

We had just arrived at the creek on a very hot Saturday morning. I looked at the bear and then pointed to show Pearl what I was looking at. Of course, she screamed and waved her flashlight. I put my hand over her mouth "Pearl! Be quiet. You will scare that poor, sad, really big bear!" The bear looked up and slowly started moving backward into the tall grass. We slowly walked toward him telling him we would help him.

Pearl immediately said, "We are really good at helping sad bears." She is such a liar! However, it did seem to calm the bear down. We handed him a piece of one of Momma's towels from our basket to dry his tears on. "What is your name? How did you get here? Where's your family, How old are you? How much do you eat, do you eat sisters?"

"Pearl!" I said, "Stop with all the questions. You are making things worse! Can't you see he has started to cry again?" I put my hand on the bear's heart and told him I could see his heart hurt. We were his friends. We would help him, and he never had to be alone and scared again.

The bear started by telling us he was 2 years old. His name was Stevie. His Momma and Daddy were with the circus. They were traveling on a train when in the middle of the night, he was jolted in his sleep by a quick stop and fell off the train. He watched as the train got further and further out of sight. He never saw his Momma or Daddy again.

He thinks it's been 3 days now that he has hidden in the tall grass. He looked hungry, Pearl said as she stepped backwards. Stevie said, "I don't eat sisters, I eat fish."

On our way back home, I told Pearl we could sneak some of Momma and Daddy's frozen fish out of the freezer. We will return tonight to feed Stevie fish for his supper.

Pearl said, "Now, how are we gonna do that, sister?"

"Well, Pearl, we are gonna take the fish out of the freezer and put it in our backpacks." She is soooo silly. Sometimes, making something so easy seem so hard.

LAZY

It was on one of these daily journeys that we met a beautiful black and white cocker spaniel. She was happily running up the street and greeted us.

Pearl whispered to me that the pup looked like a runaway. Pearl started reaching for her holster when I slapped her hand.

"You're the prettiest pup I have ever seen. Where are you headed?"

The pup smiled and said, "Anywhere but where I was. My people had me tied with a rope around a swing set. Last night, I chewed the rope and have been running since daylight."

"Well, aren't you lucky! Pearl and I were looking for a pup just like you to live with us in our home on Normal Street."

Pearl and I both had the same great idea. We could have the pup be our sister. Momma and Daddy always promised us a pup someday, and it looks like that day is here!

The little pup didn't like her name so after a few short minutes, we had one for her. Her name would be Lazy, and she wouldn't need to run anymore. She could just sleep on our bed and be 'Lazy'. The pup liked that idea and followed us home that night.

Pearl said this would be "easy peasy", talking Momma and Daddy into keeping her. Pearl made up a ridiculous story about why we should keep the pup. It was all about how we saw a house burning, and the poor little pup couldn't get out and....and well, it was just silly.

We walked into the house, and Momma and Daddy saw the pup, fell in love with her, and that's how "easy peasy" it was. No begging or crying. Pearl, the drama queen, didn't have to say a word!

Stevie and Lazy and
Harlo and Danny, Oh my!

This is where this story really begins. After Stevie, the really, really big bear, came Lazy, the cocker spaniel. After Lazy came Harlo the jack rabbit, then Danny the tortoise, then Audrey the prettiest kitty you ever saw. I would like to tell you this was all and the end of our little collection, but it was not.

Along our way, we found Betty, a black raven bird. Pockets, the tiny squirrel, and Bandit, the raccoon. Each little addition to our group of unlikely friends had a story to tell and made this the best summer ever!

We knew if we were all seen together, we would certainly be taken from one another and split up into foster homes, and there was no way that was going to happen with Betty, the black raven bird, watching over us.

We were all connected by the curiosity of two unlikely sisters and the kindred spirit they had among each other and their new friends. We would all be safe, all we needed was a plan.

"Oh no!" Pearl said she had a plan! If she does, it will include a huge, big ole story (well, a lie) and it will be so far out no one could possibly believe it. I love my little sister and will listen to her story and then pretend that I have fallen asleep. She won't wake me up because I told her to never ever wake me up unless the house is on fire. So far, she has promised not to and has kept her word.

Betty, the Black Raven Bird

Pearl and I, Stevie and Lazy, were tromping through the waters of our little creek. We didn't have galoshes for Stevie and Lazy so we were all barefoot. The cool creek water felt good on this really hot summer day. The moss was soft but slippery. At several points in our little town, the creek runs under the roads.

"This is cool," said Pearl. She loved the idea of cars going over us under the bridge and the secrecy that the people in those cars had no idea we were under them. We felt like special agents and played on this idea until almost dark most evenings.

We knew Momma and Daddy would be looking for us before it got dark so we would walk the creek until we got to the island and the Weeping Willow tree to get home hoping dark didn't set in before we got there. I would, of course, blame slow-walking Pearl, and Pearl would blame me. Whoever had the best story would be pardoned.

The bright sun was hitting our backs. Pearl said we would have a sunburn if we didn't hurry and get to the shade of the Weeping Willow tree or to the creek where the cars go over the bridge. It felt like a good day for playing spies. Stevie thought so too and Lazy didn't care, she was happy to be anywhere where there wasn't a rope.

Just as we got under the bridge, we saw a big commotion off in the distance, and a lot of birds fluttering around frantically. On the other side of the bridge was a grave yard surrounded by a heavy metal silver fence that was always padlocked. The only way in without alarming the gatekeeper was under our bridge.

Without caring what danger could lie ahead we jumped on Stevie's back and headed toward the birds. Pearl got her flashlight out (of course)! There were hundreds of dead holes with stones on them that told the stories of the people who were resting there.

Pearl started getting excited! The faster we found out what all the fuss was about, the better. I love Pearl but sometimes I think she is weird ... everything with her is a really big deal!

We found a big black Raven Bird! Her leg was a mess! She had gotten it tangled up in some of the wreaths and decorations on the dead holes.

The bird was calm, but the other birds flew away as we reached her and were worried what the humans, that dog and big bear would do to her. We explained to her that a bandage was needed to fix her up. I would be in charge of that.

Pearl tore a piece of cloth from my dress (of course!) and we started winding the cloth round and round her leg until there was a wad that looked like a ragged, dirty cast. For now, though, the black bird thought we had saved her life and was incredibly grateful. She told us she had been given the name Betty after a dead hole girl. Her mother thought she looked like a Betty. We did too!

We told Betty if she were comfortable among the dead holes where she grew up, to stay there while she healed, we would be back to check on her.

"Tomorrow is another day," Pearl said.

Harlo the Jack Rabbit

"**D**id you see that sister? Something just scared Betty, she almost lost her footing and fell over into a dead hole in the cemetery."

Pearl got quite excited. She stuck her flashlight into the air and started waving the darn thing. Gosh, really! Does she really have to do that?

"Well, Pearl, it hops, and when something hops it must be a rabbit."

As we approached the rabbit, the first thing out of Pearls mouth was, "I bet your name is Jack!"

"No, no everyone tries to call me Jack. I just don't get it! My name is Harlo and I am quick on my feet. I can run fast!!"

"Would you like to be a part of our family group?"

"Let me run for a while, and I'll get back to you tomorrow."

Pearl said we would never see him again, but there he was that very afternoon. Ready to be family.

"I just love rabbit fur coats," said Pearl.

"Don't say that ever; you will scare poor Harlo. He'll be afraid we'll skin him and make a coat!"

Here Kitty Kitty

$\mathbf{P}$earl wanted me to hold the kitty because she said her arms were all splotchy from an allergic reaction to this beautiful kitty that was as big as any dog we had ever seen! She was black and white, and her bushy tail was as long as she was. If you didn't look closely, you would have thought she was our pup, Lazy! Me and Pearl were fearful kitty would get hungry and eat our pup! (or us!)

She was feral. Even though she was sweet and just a little timid. Ok, skittish! But she still let us love on her all we wanted. She loved me, Pearl, not so much! Well, Pearl did have big blotchy red welts all over her face and arms. At best, she was a little scary looking. I couldn't blame Kitty for being skittish around her.

Pearl told me this was one animal we didn't need to rescue. Pearl the drama queen! I immediately named the kitty Audrey cause if you name something it's yours! Even Pearl had said that!

So, Audrey became ours! I always wanted a kitty and a really big kitty was the best! Besides a kitty, even a large one would be easy to hide in our little bedroom above the garage! If we could get her in the bedroom!

Boy, it would be a lot easier if Momma and Daddy had built an outside staircase to our bedroom upstairs when they built the house on Normal Street. Which, as I said before, was anything but N O R M A L!

We had to go through the garage into the laundry room and up the stairs ... which was right next to the kitchen where Momma always was cooking up something wonderful! This entry was a little dangerous because it was so close to Momma, but the other entry was through the front door, through the living room, where Daddy watched TV and then through the dining room and then the kitchen!

Either way we were doomed! If Pearl could keep them busy ... I just might be able to pull this kitty business off! But she would need to show her red splotchy spots that were now all over her body and cry her eyes out for me to pull this off! She was good at drama and she did pull it off! So did I, sneaking her upstairs!

However, as I was making my way upstairs Audrey's tail came flying out of my backpack and wiggled back and forth. It must have been 'cause she was all squished up in that backpack. I thought my knees would buckle just from the weight of her.

Once upstairs and out of the backpack she opened her mouth and started to meow when Pearl rushed over to put her hand over Audrey's mouth. My thinking was ... good move Pearl,

since I am the one who always puts my hand over her mouth! For now, we are safe with a pup and a kitty in hiding, a bird in the dead holes and Stevie, the really big bear in the dense part of the creek and woods. Our life is getting complicated!

Further down the creek there was a large dense wooded area. Our new found friends could stay there at night while Pearl, myself, and our pup Lazy and Audrey the kitty would find refuge at home. Our parents knew our imagination was pretty big for such little girls...but we weren't going to tell them about our real menagerie of new friends.

What if they believed our friends really existed....and we weren't telling just another tall tale! Riding a big ole bear seemed like something Pearl would brag about. She was kinda like that! If Pearl should change her mind and decide to tell our parents I would simply say in a very nice way...SHE IS A LIAR and that would be that. No one believed her anyway and she lied when the truth fit best!

Bandit the Noble Raccoon

& Pockets the Squirrel

Pearl had been tugging on my pretty sailor dress Momma had gotten us, she had one too. We were almost always dressed alike. Momma said we were easier to find in a crowd if we were dressed alike ... and since Pearl was always wandering off talking to strangers, I was stuck in the same garb! On this day, I didn't mind because I loved the sailor dress!

But Pearl was tugging at me, all the while talking so fast it sounded foreign! Yep! Poor pitiful Pearl was so excited. She was positive that a monkey was in the weeping willow tree on her island! Seriously... right in the middle of a small Midwestern town? But that was Pearl. She found excitement where there was none!

I looked for about an hour, holding really still so the "monkey" would make itself visible. I did see something ... it was really, really cute!

"Pearl," I said, "That's not a monkey, that's a raccoon!" Obviously, she did not know the difference between a monkey and a raccoon!

This raccoon became as interested in us as we were in him. As he climbed down off the limbs of that raggedy willow tree, he started opening up to us. Why was there such an unlikely menagerie of humans and animals together? A little girl, her sister, a big black raven bird with a dirty torn bandage on its leg? And heading up the rear of this unlikely group was a big beautiful kitty and pup and a really big bear.

I could see an explanation was needed. It started with a formal introduction." Hello Mr. Raccoon."

He interrupted and said, "Please call me Bandit ... I am not like all the other raccoons, and I like to be referenced as a common raccoon! I am of noble blood and my name is Barron, but I go by Bandit so I don't seem like a snob."

"Well then bandit, my name is Patty, this is my sister Pearl, and Betty and Lazy and Audrey and Stevie. We are all best friends. We are all going on an adventure together!"

I told Bandit it was a secret 'cause everyone in our strange little group was depending on me to tell them where the adventure was! But I didn't know where it was! I just knew that this summer would not be like any other ... and an adventure would find us.

Pockets

W e couldn't help but notice that Bandit had on a red vest, which seemed cute and at the same time kind of strange. While Pearl was chatting him up about the nobility of his bloodline and Betty kept picking at her bandage, a little ground squirrel stuck his little nose out of the pocket of Bandit's vest. You could only see the eyes and ears of this tiny little squirrel. It was the size of a mouse, and it was very skeptical of all of us. I knew this little squirrel just wished we would go away.

Bandit finally put all three legs on the ground!

Wait...1...2...3...three legs! Why did such a noble raccoon only have three legs? Should I ask what happened? Or should I just act as if all raccoons had three legs?

Nobody said a word about it. I could not believe Pearl kept her mouth shut on this one. Most of the time she is Miss Yackity Yak but this time she was as quiet as a mouse. She must be feeling sick today, because this is not the sister I know!

Bandit hobbled a little closer to us. He was pretty good at walking without a hind leg. The little squirrel hid further down into the pocket while we talked about a plan to all meet in the morning at first daylight.

"Oh gosh, we could sure use a rooster in the morning to wake us up!"

Everyone turned their back on Pearl and whispered, "what's wrong with her?" I just kept walking home with my crew following behind. Tomorrow is another day....

Danny the Tortoise

W e were all together one morning during a light summer rain. We used the tunnel under the street as shelter so we didn't get too wet. We decided we would split up today and play hide and seek among the dead holes. Off Pearl went with several of our friends, Bandit and Pockets and Audrey with her. The rest of our friends remained with me. I felt sorry for Pearl's little troupe of friends because she never quits talking! EVER!

"It's easy to win the game," said Stevie the bear. "All we need to do is follow Pearl's voice." Her team always lost this game. We gave them a head start because of Pearl. All of a sudden, we hear a frantic voice coming from the north end of the dead holes. Pearl is, as always, in a panic.

My troupe rode on Stevie's back so we could get there faster. We find a tortoise, upside down unable to move! All 4 feet stuck straight up to heaven. He is 6 feet down in a newly dug dead hole.

Pearl was screaming, "Who's gonna get him? He's gonna die! He's gonna die!"

Stevie ran to rescue the poor little tortoise who was very grateful we had come to play in the dead holes that day.

"What's your name?" asked Pearl, who is still yelling and in a terrible state of shock.

"Why my name is Danny," he said in a very low and unexcited voice. "This happens to us tortoises all the time. We fall in holes or off of a rock or street curb and unless we are found quickly or can grab onto something around us, we get stuck."

"Oh no!" said Pearl.

"Terrible," said Bandit.

"Awful," said Pockets.

Audrey, the kitty, just licked her fur and nodded.

TIME

$\mathbf{T}$ime passed, and before we even knew it the leaves were turning beautiful shades of gold, orange and purple and some of the leaves were even getting crispy and dry around our little creek. With winter coming we knew we needed to find homes for our little troupe. There would be nowhere on Normal Street to keep them.

We decided to take some pictures of our little troupe of misfits. We put them all over town in hopes someone would give them a home. We got not one person to call or send us a letter. Pearl and I were very sad about this. We wanted all of them to have a good home just like we have. What were we to do now? No way we could take them all back home. Momma and Daddy would know we had kept secrets all summer. That would be bad.

Pearl had a headache and wanted to go home early today from the creek. She wanted to get under the bed covers just like always with her stupid flashlight!

"Well Pearl, first thing, it's still daylight and why must you always want that flashlight when we talk in bed?"

A tear fell onto her cheek and she said ever so softly, "It makes me feel safe."

"Ok Pearl, but you had better quit whimpering around and help think of a great idea." I turned my head around quickly so Pearl couldn't see the tears falling on my cheeks too! Whatever are we to do?

These precious animals depend on us now and they believe we have answers for everything, but we do not. This is going to be hard, and this plan needs to happen soon! I can't stand the idea of our new friends being homeless and helpless and what would be worse, separated and scared. They are our family now!

As we laid our heads down on our cozy, safe pillows, I told Pearl I was coming down with the sniffles, so I turned my head away from her and started to sob. I couldn't fool Pearl. She said my sniffles sounded more like a heartache. It did and it was. Sometimes my little sister surprises me.

Days go By

Autumn days went by faster than summer days. Maybe it felt that way 'cause we were so upset about where our animal friends would go. The big tent would be going up for the revival soon. It would be the last time this year before cold weather sets in.

Our little group enjoyed looking under that darn old tent last summer so Pearl and I decided to take them for the last revival of the year.

"Maybe the last ever! Ever," screamed Pearl as she put her head down and tears fell on her bare feet. All of a sudden, Pearl lifted her head with a big smile. She had a great silly idea.

"Let's dress them up and make it a party. We can get clothes down from the attic, I can use my flashlight and get Momma's and Daddy's nice dress clothes out of the summer trunk. We will dress them up and they will be beautiful. We'll get jewelry from Momma's pretty box on her dresser."

"Ok Pearl!" I said, "Now you are going way too far with this pet masquerade. We will not take our mother's beautiful jewelry out of that box. That's going way too far even for me. I can just see you putting an earring on Audrey the kitty and she would run with that earring like that costume jewelry was real and that would be the end of Audrey. Pearl, Daddy bought that jewelry for Mama. They are just pretty glass earrings but to our beautiful Mama they all were real diamonds and you, my dear little sister, will not take them! Do you understand Pearl?"

Pearl agreed but I don't trust anyone who carries a flashlight in a holster everywhere they go. Laying out clothes for our little troupe was easy. Mama and Daddy had lots of great stuff in the old trunks in the attic. They both dressed up when they went dancing on most Saturday nights. That's when Pearl and I would pilfer. We would dress up and be everything from a cook in a diner to a princess in a far away land! Our little menagerie was going to be dressed to the nines! That means *awesome*.

We decided our little pup Lazy would be wearing a beautiful red scarf with a purple brooch.

Stevie had a jacket with buttons that didn't really button at all. Bandit had black silk pants and an orange tie.

We painted the tortoise Danny with blue and white polka dots on his back and on the other side we painted the words Danny is family. He really liked that.

Audrey the kitty had a white satin bow tied around her neck and tail.

Betty being a bird with a limp got a large silver nail to use as her crutch. Pearl found a fancy marble to put on top of her nail. The marble is called a cat eye. I thought that was rather cruel but Pearl got her way and the marble was glued on top of the nail. It was a pretty walking-stick. Betty was also wearing a pretty yellow blouse from our dolls closet. It looked great with her black feathers.

Harlo dressed in a black and white striped jacket from our doll's drawer and a little black ball cap with a picture of a Barbie Doll on it.

Pockets wasn't having any of this dressing up business and stayed tucked inside Bandit's vest. Everyone was now dressed and beautifully coiffured and the men all looked dapper.

Pearl and I could not be outdone by our new friends, so Pearl put on a pair of sunglasses. She'll need that cause her stupid flashlight is so bright. She also wore a pair of diamond-like earrings with a matching necklace.

I wore Daddy's black silk top hat and a pink and black polka dot bow tie with a pink box pleated skirt. I also found a pair of sky high, high heels. Pearl was more than a little put off she couldn't find any heels to fit her tiny feet. I felt kind of bad for her. Well, not really. Now we were all ready for our next adventure.

Pearl had no idea I sort of had a plan with all of this fussing around in the attic looking through our trunks. Telling her would have been a disaster. She would have secretly told everyone and gotten their hopes up for a home that might never ever happen. Quietly we all walked to the tent. One by one we lifted the edge of the canvas to see what was going on under the large tent. Revivals can be entertaining and loud. Sneaking peaks was more fun than if we had had front row seats. The fun is all about not getting caught!

What we hadn't counted on was a security guard taking a smoke. We never thought about anyone finding us with our butts sticking up towards the heavens.

The security guard blew his whistle. We all stood up at attention since I looked as though I had a place of authority with my top hat, so I spoke up. Kind of like the ringleader of this group of very interesting-looking misfits.

I told the security guard that we were in fact the entertainment for the evening. When he blew his whistle, at that very minute, I heard our cue to enter the arena. So off we must go! I told the guard thank you for watching over us as we waited for our turn to go into the revival under the big top.

Pearl said, "That was genius, big top sounded so professional." I can only think of one thing now, what are we gonna do when we get in there?

$\mathbf{M}$aybe a higher power was in that tent that night, but all of a sudden like a bolt of lightning it hit me. Since we were showing our little friends a good time, I'll use this moment to take sour lemons and make lemonade.

So, we marched single file, except for Pearl, who was riding on my shoulders, waving that silly flashlight as she always does when she gets excited. We did look impressive.

I reached over and got the microphone from the choir leader and said "Good evening ladies and gentlemen and children."

You could hear a pin drop; it was so quiet. You should have seen the look on both Pearl and the minister's faces. I wanted to laugh but no one said a word because the people putting on the revival wanted to look as if they knew what was going to happen. It's called saving face.

Actually, they had no idea of what was going to happen after the introduction. I told the townspeople that a raffle was going to take place on this very night and how very lucky they chose this night to attend.

This raffle was being done to find each and every one of these fabulous animals a winter home and that all the money collected would go to keep them fed and warm in the winter and to keep them from being homeless and hungry. The worst of all would be having them get sick with the SHIVERS.

Everyone was so excited they had never seen such beautiful costumes on so many animals before. The people in the tent started waving their hands with fists full of money as they yelled out which animals they wanted.

But when Betty the bird hobbled forward with tears running down her beak, she struggled to get her words out. She started speaking "But, but we will all be separated and scared and lonely without each other, we are all a family."

As she spoke, each and every one of the ladies and gentlemen cried big tears. Again, on that chilly fall night a higher power took over the minister and as he stood up cleared his throat and wiped the tears from his eyes.

He said, "Now, now, there will be none of that in this revival tonight. We will keep all of them together and they will travel with us to warm sunny places during the cold winter months. We will keep them warm and happy and fed. They will always have a home with us."

That minister was pretty darn smart. He knew that Pearl and my little group would bring in a larger crowd wherever they went. Which meant the money that they collected would be greater than they had ever seen or dreamed of.

Pearl had a lot of under the covers, bedtime flashlight talk that night! But I was excited and willing to listen to her ramble on and on. She asked if I had planned that all along for our beautiful animal friends?

"Well yes, of course!" I said, "When you are a genius you just don't give away your secrets." Now that Pearl believes that little story, maybe she will quit the yackety-yak and listen to me for a change.

Tomorrow the revival packs up the tent and the chairs along with our menagerie of friends of whom we shared the best summer ever with and leaves our little town. They will return in the spring and again in the summer and fall. We will still have good times with them while they are here for the big tent revival.

We will cry big Stevie bear tears. He taught us how to do that, as we wave goodbye. Our hearts will hurt but knowing we will see them again and they have a good home makes Pearl and I happy! Oh! I took the batteries out of Pearls flashlight.
Love Patty.

P.S. I can't wait to see what our next adventure will be. I will turn nine years old and Pearl will be five. She thinks she's already 13! What 13-year-old carries a flashlight? NONE!

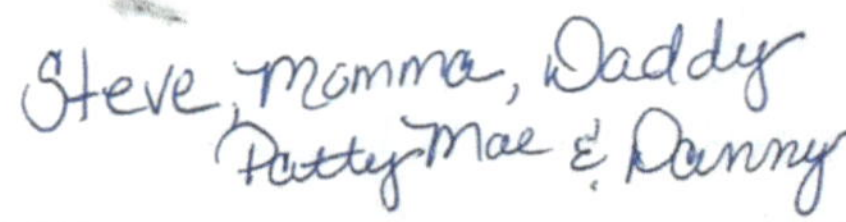

Danny & Lazy

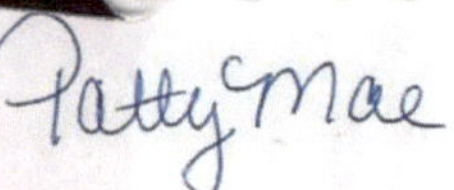

Patty Mae

Momma (Audrey) Patricia (Patty Mae)
Danny & Steve

43